# Grassland Scientists

By Patrick and Janet Lalley

STECK-VAUGHN
ELEMENTARY • SECONDARY • ADULT • LIBRARY
A Harcourt Company

www.steck-vaughn.com

**ISBN 0-7398-4937-9**



Printed and bound in the United States of America
1 2 3 4 5 6 7 8 9 10 WZ 05 04 03 02 01

**Photo Acknowledgments**
Corbis, 9, 25, 36, 39
Digital Stock, 10, 11, 22, 40 (bottom); 41 (top and bottom)
Ordway Memorial Prairie, cover, 26, 30
Photo Network/Dennis Junor, 9
Photophile/Norton Photography, 6; Doug Wilson, 32
South Dakota Tourism, title page, 40 (top), 44; Chad Coppess Photography, 28
Visuals Unlimited/Jana R. Jirak, 17

**Content Consultants**
Maria Kent Rowell
Science Consultant
Sebastopol, California

David Larwa
National Science Education Consultant
Educational Training Services
Brighton, Michigan

**This book supports the National Science Standards.**

# Contents

This map shows where grasslands are located throughout the world.

# What Is a Grasslands Biome?

Many scientists study the grasslands **biome**. A biome is a large region, or area, made of communities. A community is a group of certain plants and animals that live in the same place.

Communities in the same biome are alike in some ways. In the grasslands, for example, plants and animals must be able to live in large open areas without many trees.

Scientists call grasslands a **transitional biome**. That means they are usually found between two other biomes. Grasslands are usually located between forests and deserts.

Grasslands are found on every continent except Antarctica. Most grasslands are on the continents of North America, Africa, and Asia.

Pampas grass can grow more than 12 feet (4 m) tall. It grows on tall or mixed grasslands.

## Kinds of Grasslands

The three types of grasslands are tall, mixed, and short grasslands. Grasses on tall grasslands can grow up to 15 feet (4.6 m) tall. Mixed grasslands have grasses that grow 2 to 3 feet

(0.6 to 0.9 m) tall. Grasses in the short grasslands are about 2 feet (0.6 m) tall.

All three types of grasslands grow in the United States, where they are commonly called prairies. In Africa, Australia, and Asia, grasslands are often called savannas.

## What Are Grasslands?

Grasslands are large areas where many kinds of grasses grow. Grasslands have widely ranging temperatures. They are very hot in the summer, and they become much colder in the winter.

Different types of grasslands receive different amounts of rain. The tall-grass areas receive almost 30 inches (75 cm) of rain each year. The mixed-grass areas receive 15 to 25 inches (38 to 63 cm) each year. The short-grass areas receive less than 10 inches (25 cm) of rain each year.

Grasslands have rich topsoil. Topsoil is the dark dirt that sits on the surface. It provides many **nutrients** for plants. Nutrients are materials that living things need to stay healthy and to grow.

## What Plants Live on Grasslands?

Grassland plants have **adapted** to live in grassy areas with hot and cold seasons. To be adapted means that something is a good fit for where it lives. Many of the plants that live in grasslands could not live in another biome.

Many different types of grasses and **wildflowers** grow on grasslands. A common type of grass is called buffalo grass. Like many grassland grasses, it grows quickly and needs little water to survive. Few trees or shrubs grow on the grasslands. There is too much wind and not enough water for them to grow.

**FUN FACT**

Did you know a lawn can be made from wild grassland plants? A mixture of wild grasses, such as buffalo grass and blue grama, can become a lawn for people's homes. Wild grasses grow only a few inches high and rarely need watering.

Most grasslands have no trees or shrubs growing on them.

Meerkats are small mammals that live on the savannas of Africa.

## What Animals Live on Grasslands?

The grasslands are home to many kinds of animals. Many grassland animals are mammals. A mammal is a warm-blooded animal with a backbone. Warm-blooded animals have a body temperature that stays the same even when it is hot or cold outside.

Small grassland mammals include prairie dogs, meerkats, black-footed ferrets, and mice. Larger grassland mammals, such as buffalo and coyotes, live on the prairie in North America. In Africa, grassland mammals include lions, zebras, giraffes, and elephants.

Did you know that there were once millions of buffalo? In the mid-1800s, there were more than 60 million buffalo, or bison, living wild in the prairie grasslands. What happened to them? As people settled in the American West, they killed the buffalo for sport, for food, for their hides, or to clear them off the land for farming.

## How and Why Global Warming Happens

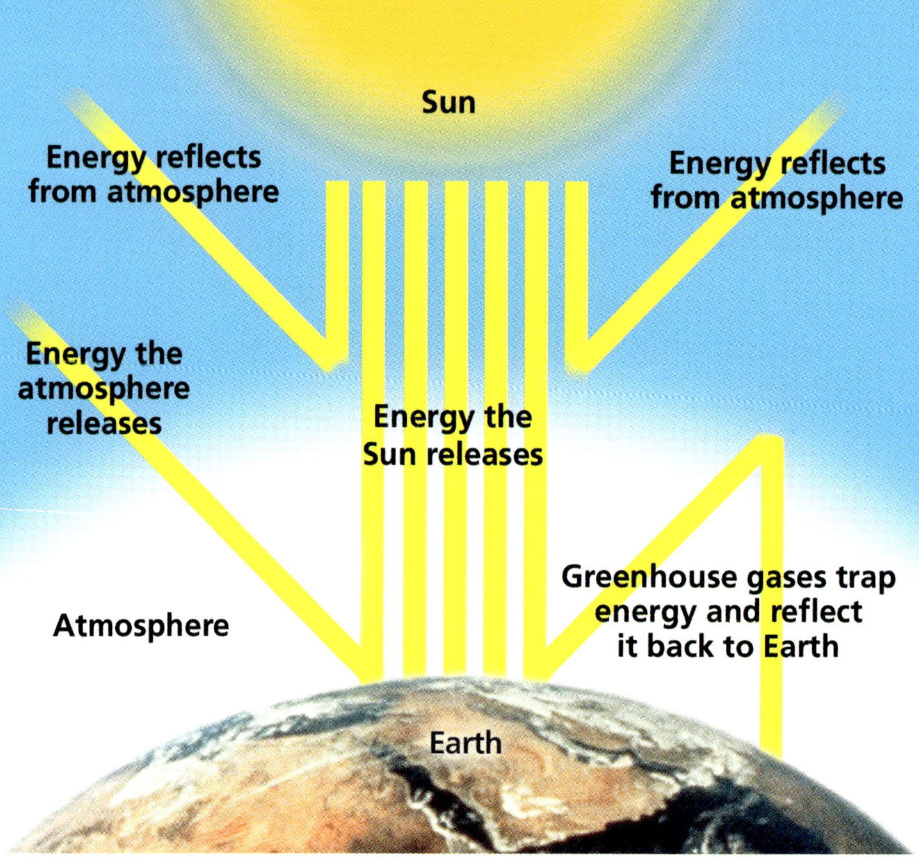


## Why Are the Grasslands in Danger?

Natural grasslands are rare. Since the invention of the steel plow, many native grasslands have been turned into farmland. People have done this because the soil on the grasslands is so rich in nutrients. Farmers can grow many kinds of crops in what was once grassland soil. As people replace the grasslands, they hurt native habitats. A habitat is a place where an animal or plant usually lives. Once their habitat is destroyed, the wild animals have to leave and find new homes.

Farms also have many animals. Many people who raise livestock, or animals used for food, eat the native grasslands. With fewer grasses on the grasslands, wind and water can carry away the healthy soil. This is called erosion. During dry times, the wind can cause dust storms because there are not enough grasses to hold soil in place.

Global warming can also affect grasslands. Global warming is a slow but measurable rise in temperatures across all of Earth. Even small changes in temperatures can cause changes in weather patterns. These changes mean some grasslands might receive more or less rain than they used to. Some might have higher or lower temperatures. New weather patterns may affect or even hurt some grassland plants and animals.

New grasslands sometimes form. When people clear forests for farms, and then stop farming after the soil is no longer healthy, the land that was once a forest can become a savanna.

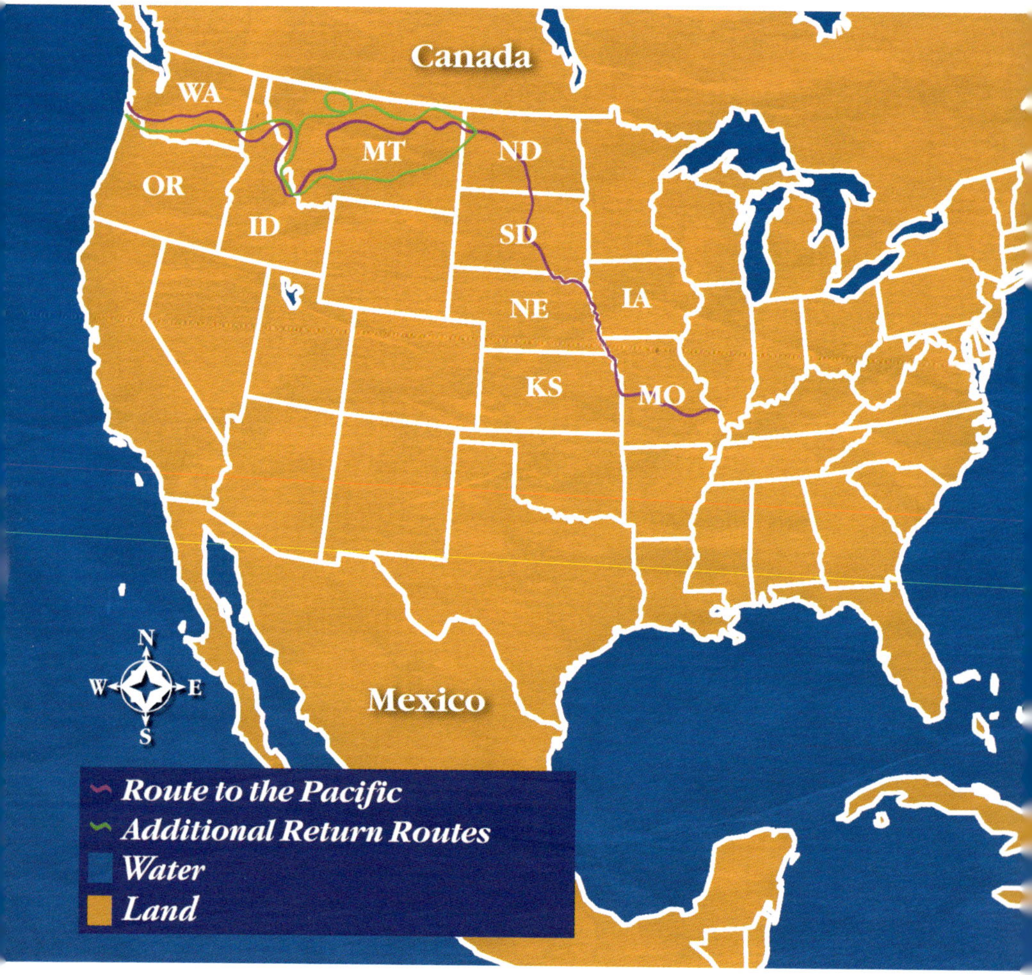


This map shows the path of Lewis and Clark's journey through the American West.

# Scientists of the Old American West

Meriwether Lewis and William Clark are two of the most famous explorers in the history of the United States. But they were more than explorers. They also gave the scientific world the first look at the **American West**.

President Thomas Jefferson sent the two men on a two-year trip to explore a huge piece of land he bought from France in 1803. The land was called the Louisiana Purchase. Today, that land is the middle section of the United States. Beginning in 1804, Lewis, Clark, and their traveling companions journeyed by boat up the Missouri River. Surrounding the middle parts of the Missouri River they saw thousands of miles of the grasslands now called the Great Plains.

## What Did Lewis and Clark Find?

In 1804, most of the people living in the Great Plains were Native Americans. Lewis and Clark did not know what they would find when they left St. Louis. They had about 20 other men with them. They called themselves the Corps of Discovery.

Lewis and Clark wrote down everything they saw and learned in their journals. They also sent President Jefferson many messages. They even sent him some live animals, including prairie dogs. Scientists in the United States and Europe had never seen a prairie dog. There were many animals along the Missouri River that people from the East had never seen. Pronghorn antelope, coyotes, and jackrabbits were all new to them.

Lewis and Clark also found many new plants. They spent the winter with Native Americans in what is now North Dakota. One of their traveling companions returned home to take their journals to the president. They had written 45,000 words. The companion also brought back seeds, plants, and live animals to the president.

**Lewis and Clark were the first to write about prairie dogs.**

President Jefferson was excited about what Lewis and Clark had found. He planted some of the seeds and told other scientists about all the new animals. People were amazed by Lewis and Clark's journals. They added a lot to the world's knowledge about nature.

## After the Expedition

Lewis and Clark's expedition helped to change the United States. People began to move to the new land Lewis and Clark had written about. They also began to take the land that had belonged to the Native Americans. It took only about 100 years for the **settlers** to take almost all of the Native Americans' land.

The new settlers also hunted the animals in the prairie. They killed almost all the buffalo there. In the early 1800s, Lewis and Clark saw bears and elk in the prairie. No bears or elk live there anymore. Farmers also began to plow the land to plant crops. As a result, there are not very many places where native grasses grow today.

The journals of Lewis and Clark tell us what the prairie was like before it was settled. Their journals are called one of the greatest natural histories ever written. The seeds Lewis and Clark sent back grew into plants. The plants are still on display today at Jefferson's old home in Virginia.

This drawing shows William Clark handing out presents to Native Americans.

This map shows where the Serengeti National Park is in Tanzania, Africa.

# A Scientist on the Serengeti

Samuel J. McNaughton is a scientist who works in the Serengeti National Park in Africa. He has been studying the savanna there for 27 years. Serengeti National Park is as big as Connecticut and New Hampshire put together. McNaughton says that most people think Africa is hot all the time. But it is hot in the sun and cool in the shade. "At night you sleep under a blanket," McNaughton says.

McNaughton likes the savannas because they are beautiful and can be dangerous. Elephants could charge toward people at any time. McNaughton says the most dangerous animal is the siafu ant. Siafus come out at night. They appear in groups of millions, and one group can eat an animal as big as a cape buffalo.

Poachers often kill rhinoceroses that live on savannas to sell the horns.

## What Does McNaughton Do?

Savannas have more large mammals than any other place on Earth. Large mammals have lived on savannas for millions of years. McNaughton wants to find out how so many different kinds of large mammals can live there.

When something happens to a plant or animal because of a change, it affects the rest of the living things in the savanna. McNaughton does experiments by changing the savannas in small ways. He may set up fences to keep the animals in one place. Sometimes he adds things to the soil or adds water to an area. Then, he writes down the results of his experiments.

McNaughton has observed poaching. Poaching means to hunt an animal when it against the law to do so. Poachers can make a lot of money by selling the animals they kill. McNaughton has seen how poachers kill animals and change the savanna. The savanna can change so much, that it will not even be a savanna anymore. That is because the other living things in the savanna need the animals that the poachers kill in order to survive. Without them, other animals and plants could die, too.

## Keeping Savannas Healthy

McNaughton says the most important thing scientists can do is publish their findings so other people can read them. He says it does not matter what scientists find out until they let other people know about it.

When visitors enter the Serengeti National Park, they receive a brochure that teaches them about the park. Much of the information in the brochure comes from McNaughton. "My knowledge becomes part of the visitor's knowledge," McNaughton says. The visitors can pass that knowledge on to someone else.

McNaughton believes the savannas can survive a long time. "If they are properly managed, they have a bright future," he says. But people have to stop interfering with the savannas. They have to stop poaching and polluting the land.

These visitors to Serengeti National Park are going on a safari to learn about the savanna.

This scientist at the Ordway Memorial Prairie is studying ways to keep the grasses healthy.

# A Scientist on the Prairie

Mary C. Miller is the manager of the Ordway Memorial Prairie in northeast South Dakota. Thousands of buffalo once lived on the prairie in North and South Dakota. Then settlers came and built farms, and almost all of the buffalo died. The Ordway Memorial Prairie is a park where the land is kept the way it used to be.

Miller says that the prairie can be a hard place to work. "In the winter, it is very cold. We get a lot of snow and **blizzards**," she says. "In the summer, it is hot, and sometimes there are **tornadoes**. The wind blows most of the time. Sometimes the wind blows so hard, a person can barely walk."

This is a planned fire that Miller started to keep the Ordway Memorial Prairie healthy.

## What Does Miller Do?

Miller spends a lot of time alone studying prairie plants and animals. One day, she was at a wetland counting birds. A wetland is any type of small lake or marsh. "A large shorebird with a long bill, called a Marbled Godwit, flew over," she says. "It started swooping and diving at my head. The bird had a nest nearby and was trying to protect it. The bird did not know I would never hurt its nest."

Miller goes to the library to look for information to help answer her questions. She also talks to other scientists and does experiments when no one knows the answer. "I will keep reading, talking, and doing experiments until I have answers to my questions. I would like to know about how plants react when they are grazed by bison and how insects, birds, and mammals use plants for cover and food."

Wildfires once raced across the prairie. People do not usually think of fire as a good thing, but many prairie plants are helped by regular fires. The fires were part of nature. The plants and animals needed them to survive. Miller now starts fires on purpose to manage the prairie, but digs trenches to make sure they do not spread to farms or towns.

Farms and towns take up most of the land in the prairie. Buffalo once roamed all over it. Today, buffalo still live on the Ordway Memorial Prairie.

These buffalo live on the Ordway Memorial Prairie and eat the grasses that grow there.

## Keeping Prairies Healthy

Miller says we need to have prairies to understand how one thing affects another. "The bison living in the prairie feed on the many grasses. While the buffalo eats the grass, the bison also helps to make more plants. The seeds may stick to the bison's coat and fall off in a new place. As the bison walk around, they push plant seeds into the ground with their hooves. When the seeds are pushed into the ground, they are able to grow."

This kind of science helps people learn new things. "It is put into action all over the world," says Miller. But learning these things is not easy. "Much of the prairie where I work has been plowed or is being invaded by weeds," she says.

"We keep learning new information about how to keep the prairie healthy. The prairie is so big and open, it makes a person feel very small. The prairie is full of contrasts. It has very harsh weather, but very delicate creatures and plants live in the prairie. I believe that if people work together to protect the remaining prairies and work to restore the prairies that have been lost, then the prairies will be here for many years to come."

Some scientists try to save grasslands by studying the best ways to grow grass plants.

# What Does the Future Hold for Grasslands?

The future of grasslands depends on people. Many grasslands are in danger of being used by people for farms, ranches, or homes. They can be saved, though, by preventing further damage to them.

Areas that were once grasslands can also be replanted. Native grasses and wildflowers can be planted on land that was being used to raise crops or to graze livestock. Over time, these plants will grow and the land will become a grassland again.

People can help grasslands by not stopping grassland wildfires. These fires allow the grasslands to be free of trees and shrubs. The plants in the grasslands have adapted to fires.

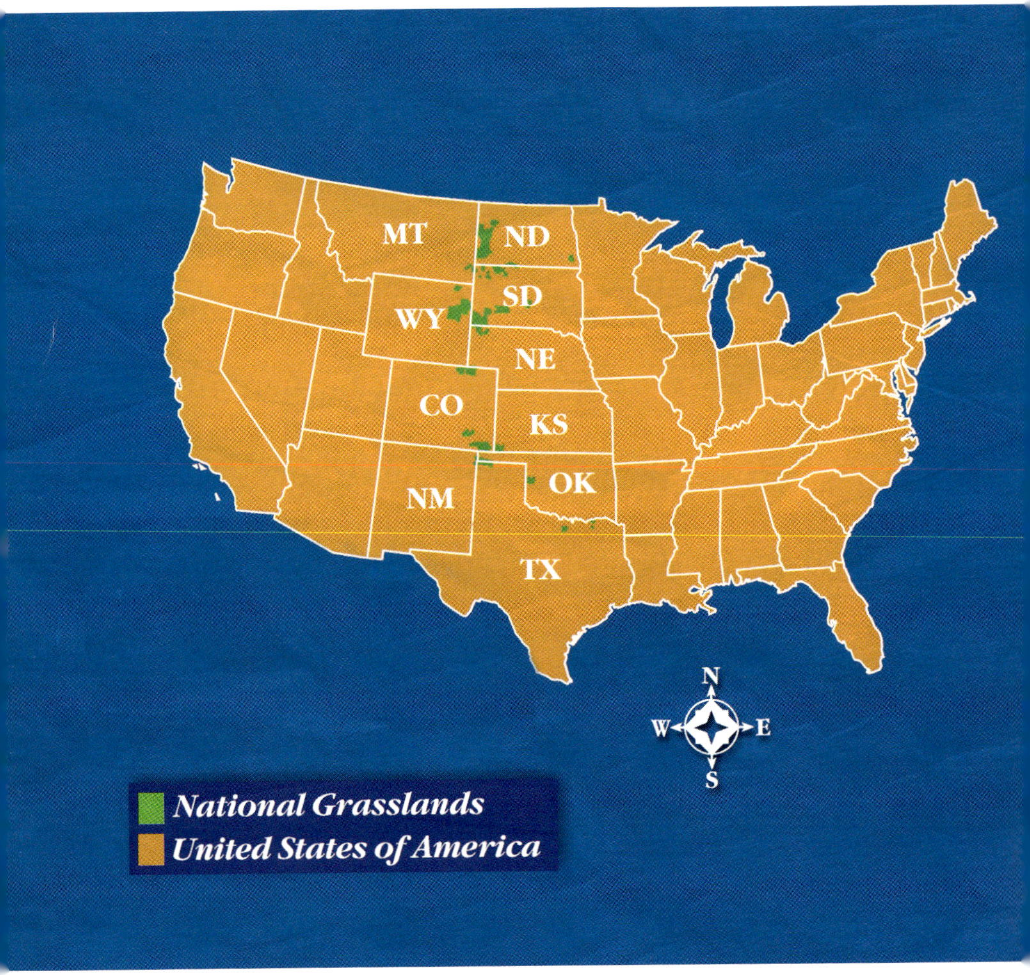


This map shows where the national grasslands are in the United States.

## Where Are Grasslands Protected Best?

Grasslands are protected best in national parks. A national park is a park that is owned and protected by the government. The managers of these parks prevent people from damaging the natural plants and animals. They also make sure that pollution does not harm the grasslands.

Park managers can also make sure that all the plants and animals needed for the **food chain** are there. A food chain is a group of animals and plants that eat each other to survive. Each animal or plant feeds on the one below it in the chain. If the food chain is not broken, animal and plant numbers stay healthy and controlled.

There are several national grasslands in the United States. The largest of these is the Little Missouri National Grassland in North Dakota. The park has more than 1 million acres (404,690 ha). The smallest is the McClelland Creek National Grassland in Texas. It has 1,449 acres (586 ha).

There are very few black-footed ferrets left living in the wild grasslands.

## The Endangered Black-Footed Ferret

One endangered grassland animal is the black-footed ferret. Endangered means the animal is in danger of becoming extinct. The black-footed ferret is one of the rarest mammals in North America. There are few of them left in their natural habitat. Most of the black-footed ferrets alive today are kept in captivity by people trying to help them.

The black-footed ferret eats prairie dogs and needs them to survive. As the number of prairie dogs has decreased, so has the number of black-footed ferrets. Prairie dogs are killed by people in every state in which they live. People consider them pests. Without prairie dogs to eat, the ferrets continue to struggle to survive.

Over the past several years, ferrets born in captivity have been brought back to native grassland areas. Many of these ferrets have been killed by coyotes or badgers. Some, though, have survived, and scientists continue to release more each year.

## What Can You Do to Save Ferrets?

Black-footed ferrets need people's help to survive. You can write letters to the governors of Montana, Wyoming, South Dakota, and Colorado, asking them to protect ferret habitats.

To protect ferrets, people will also have to protect prairie dogs. You can also help by contacting one of the groups with an address or website listed in the back of this book. These groups help to teach people about saving the black-footed ferret and other **species**. They also teach people about how to save the habitat ferrets and other species live in.

### What Are Other Kids Saying?

Sarah Brubeck is a 13-year-old student who believes people should work to save grasslands because of the animals. She says, "Think about it. Weren't they here first? They were here millions of years before us, and then when we come, we start cutting down their homes and making our homes. We need our space, and they need their space."

These scientists are releasing a black-footed ferret into the wild.

# Quick Facts

During dry times, grasses on grasslands can become dormant, meaning they stop growing. These grasses will stay dormant until it rains again.

Some grasslands in Asia are also called steppes.

Some grasslands in South Africa are also called veldts.

Some grasslands in Africa are also called savannas.

The soil on African savannas is often red.

The poaching of savanna animals, including the elephant and rhinoceros, has put many of them in danger of dying out.

U.S. farmland that was once wild prairie is known as the "breadbasket of the world." It is called this because the crops grown there make up a huge part of the world's food supply.

Owls and hawks are birds that live on prairie grasslands. Hawks and owls are predators, meaning they hunt other animals and eat them for food.

On the following pages, you can find sources of information that tell how to help save grasslands.

# Glossary

**adapt** (uh-DAPT)—to change in order to survive

**American West** (uh-MER-uh-kuhn WEST)—the area generally west of the Mississippi River in the United States explored by early settlers and explorers

**biome** (BYE-ohm)—large regions, or areas, in the world that have similar climates, soil, plants, and animals

**blizzard** (BLIZ-urd)—a severe snowstorm

**food chain** (FOOD CHAYN)—an ordered arrangement of animals and plants in which each feeds on the one below it

**nutrient** (NOO-tree-uhnt)—something that is needed by living things to grow and to stay healthy and strong

**settlers** (SET-lurz)—people who are among the first to make their homes in a new country or territory

**species** (SPEE-seez)—one of the groups into which animals and plants are divided according to their features; members of the same species can mate and have young

**tornado** (tor-NAY-doh)—a strong storm of winds that rotate

**transitional biome** (tran-ZISH-uhn-al BYE-ome)—a biome that is usually found between two other biomes

**wildflower** (WILDE-flou-ur)—a native flowering plant that grows and spreads by itself, without human help

# Internet Sites

**Biomes/Habitats**

http://www.allaboutnature.com/biomes

*Find a description of each biome and information about the exciting animals that live there.*

**Children of the Earth United**

http://childrenoftheearth.org/

*Learn things you can do to help improve the environment.*

**EEK! Environmental Education for Kids**

http://www.dnr.state.wi.us/org/caer/ce/eek/index.htm

*Discover different problems facing the environment and some ways to help solve them.*

**Lady Bird Johnson Wildflower Center**

http://www.wildflower.org/forchildren.html

*See and learn about different flowers and plants that grow on the grasslands of the United States.*

# Useful Addresses

**Center for Plant Conservation**
c/o Missouri Botanical Garden
P.O. Box 299
St. Louis, MO 61366

**National Audubon Society**
700 Broadway
New York, NY 10003

**Nature Conservancy**
1815 North Lynn Street
Arlington, VA 22209

**Tallgrass Prairie National Preserve**
P.O. Box 585
Cottonwood Falls, KS 66845

# Books to Read

**Hirschi, Ron.** *Save Our Prairies and Grasslands.* New York: Delacorte, 1994.

*Learn about problems facing prairies and grasslands and different ways to save them.*

**Horton, Catherine.** *A Closer Look at Grasslands.* New York: Gloucester, 1979.

*Discover the different plants and animals that live on grasslands.*

**Johnson, Rebecca.** *A Walk in the Prairie.* Minneapolis: Carolrhoda, 2000.

*This book describes the different things you would see if you took a walk around a prairie.*

**Silver, Donald.** *African Savanna.* New York: McGraw Hill, 1997.

*Learn all about the animals, climate, and conservation problems of the savannas.*

# Index